SPORTS INJURY

Prevention and First Aid Management

The Companion Manual for the
National Coaching Foundation Key Course

ISBN 1 85060 168 2

Published jointly by:

The Scottish Sports Council, copyright © 1991
Caledonia House
South Gyle
Edinburgh
EH12 9DQ
Telephone: 031-317 7200
Fax: 031-317 7202

St Andrew's Ambulance Association, copyright © 1991
St Andrew's House
Milton Street
Glasgow
G4 0HR
Telephone: 041-332 4031
Fax: 041-332 6582

The National Coaching Foundation, copyright © 1991
4 College Close
Beckett Park
Leeds
LS6 3QH
Telephone: 0532-744 802
Fax: 0532-755 019

Trade distribution by
Coachwise Ltd.
4 College Close
Beckett Park
Leeds
LS6 3QH

Typesetting and Design by Type Aligne
West Coates House
90 Haymarket Terrace
Edinburgh
EH12 5LQ
Telephone: 031-337 6570
Fax:: 031-337 6518

Printed and Bound by Holmes McDougall, Edinburgh

CONTENTS

FOREWORD

Injuries can happen when exercising or during sport. This book is for all those involved in exercise and sport – the participant, the parent, the teacher, the coach and the official. It provides a ready guide to injury prevention and First Aid management. These are everyone's responsibility.

There is, however, no substitute for practical training, and you should attend a recognised First Aid course to supplement the advice offered in this book. As well as the more general First Aid qualifications offered by St Andrew's Ambulance Association, St John Ambulance and the British Red Cross Society, there is now a First Aid course specifically designed to meet the needs of sport. This is Sports Injury: Prevention and First Aid Management, which has been developed by St Andrew's Ambulance Association, the National Coaching Foundation and the Scottish Sports Council. This handbook provides the basis of the course material and is presented in six main sections, each denoted by different coloured page borders.

NOTE

The Manual can be used as a guideline for treatment by the untrained. However, the lifesaving techniques of Artificial Ventilation and External Chest Compression and the techniques for the management of Spinal Injuries should not be used until you have received proper instructions from a qualified instructor.

Section

1

SPORTS INJURY

2 INTRODUCTION/FIT TO PARTICIPATE

INTRODUCTION

More and more people of all ages are now exercising regularly for the benefit of their health. Regular exercise is not a substitute for an unhealthy lifestyle. Being overweight, smoking, taking drugs or excess alcohol is harmful to health.

For many people exercise and sport can be fun. Everyone is different and when planning an exercise programme, age, current fitness level, aims, personal ability and time available must be considered.

If participants try to do too much too soon, they are more likely to sustain an injury. A well planned programme, combined with a sound knowledge of safe practice, will help to develop fitness and avoid injury.

Should injuries occur, prompt and appropriate treatment will minimise damage, help to achieve a quick and safe return to activity and reduce the likelihood of the injury recurring.

FIT TO PARTICIPATE?

General fitness refers to the overall physical condition of the individual and can range from illness through good health to the peak of human condition.

Fitness is affected by a number of factors - age, lifestyle, training, illness and injury, physical and psychological state, diet and rest. Individuals have considerable control over their own health and level of fitness.

A carefully planned exercise programme will readily maintain or improve an individual's general fitness. This might take no more than an hour a week for the average participant.

If you wish to improve your all-round fitness the type of exercise you adopt must make your heart, lungs, muscles and joints work hard eg cycling, swimming, running, jogging, badminton, skipping and brisk walking. The most enjoyable way to exercise and improve your overall health, is to try and take part in one or two different sports each week. This will keep a different range of muscles and joints active while improving the efficiency of your heart and lungs.

In addition to active exercise you should also consider spending ten minutes a day doing exercises to improve joint flexibility and muscle strength. Remember the older you are the more you will benefit.

Overall fitness consists of four main components:

- endurance (stamina);
- strength;
- flexibility; and
- speed.

These four components are required in varying proportions for different forms of exercise and sport. For example, cyclists need a high level of endurance, gymnasts need good strength and flexibility, sprinters need speed and strength.

STARTING OUT

Whatever the level of participation start slowly and build up gradually.

All too often people rush into a new exercise or training programme, and allow their eagerness to override their common sense. The importance of a step by step approach is essential. This is just as true for experienced athletes as for older participants or youngsters who are developing their fitness or sporting potential.

Any exercise programme should allow adequate time for rest and relaxation. Recuperation is an important part of training.

DIET AND SPORT

It is not necessary to have a special diet if you are involved in sport[1]. Everyone, whatever their level of activity, should eat a well balanced diet, avoiding the common error of eating too much fat and not enough carbohydrate. Carbohydrates are the main fuel supply used by muscles during activity and the best sources of this type of food are bread, pasta, potatoes and rice.

Accordingly, it is possible to plan a training programme for any individual by blending the four main fitness components, depending on the chosen activity.

Footnote

1   For further information on diet and sport, the National Coaching Foundation course on "Nutrition and Sports Performance" is strongly recommended (see p80).

During exercise the body loses fluid through evaporation and sweat. Therefore it is essential that athletes in training and competition drink large amounts of fluid such as water, diluted fruit juice and tea to compensate for this loss.

HAZARDS IN ACTIVE EXERCISE

Active exercise can, and will, do harm in three main sets of circumstances.

First of all, too much exercise too soon in a training programme can lead to injury.

Secondly, injury or illness can occur when the individual is training vigorously, to the very limits of his or her capability. Under this kind of pressure the body structure can fail.

Thirdly, irrespective of the stage of your training programme, your level of fitness or your sport, you will suffer injury if you use inappropriate, poor quality equipment and do not clearly understand the basic rules of the activity in which you are participating. This warning particularly applies to footwear. For example, disaster will strike if you attempt to climb Ben Nevis in training shoes on a cold, wet, windy winter's day. Likewise, lower leg injuries are more likely to occur running a marathon in gym shoes rather than training shoes designed for distance running.

Section 2

PREVENTION

AND

REDUCTION

OF
INJURIES
AND ILLNESSES
IN SPORT

CAUSES OF INJURY IN SPORT

Injuries happen in sport no matter how much care is taken and despite advances in equipment, medicine and coaching. Injuries occur most frequently in:

- high risk activities (eg downhill skiing);
- contact sports (eg rugby); and
- sports making extreme demands on muscle strength (eg weightlifting).

Injuries are more likely to occur in poor conditions, for example extremes of temperature, wind, rain and poor light. The most common injuries affect the soft tissues (skin, muscle, ligament, tendon), the bones and the joints. Less common but potentially more serious injuries can occur to the internal organs (brain, spinal cord, chest and abdominal organs).

There are two principle causes of injury:

- direct or extrinsic – as the result of a fall or blow, and
- indirect or intrinsic – when tissues break down or become inflamed as a result of repeated stress or overuse. The indirect injury usually results from poor technique, unsuitable equipment, inappropriate training programmes, overtraining, or poor practice procedures.

CAUSES OF ILLNESS IN SPORT

ENVIRONMENTAL FACTORS

Changes in environmental conditions can make inappropriately equipped people and even highly trained athletes more prone to illness.

Illnesses which can arise from changes in environmental conditions include:

- **hypothermia** (dangerous lowering of body temperature) from exposure to extreme cold and inclement weather (wind and rain);
- **heat exhaustion** from high temperatures and dehydration;
- **mountain sickness** (oxygen reduction) at high altitudes; and
- **the bends** (nitrogen decompression sickness) from too rapid a reduction in pressure after exposure to high pressures (eg deep sea diving).

Individuals should never participate in vigorous exercise and sport if they have a **temperature or flu-like symptoms**. Any participant in sport, but especially veterans, must seek medical advice if undue breathlessness or chest pains develop while exercising. It is important that parents, teachers and coaches are aware of these risks.

OVERTRAINING

Overtraining will result in ill-health as well as loss of form and increased likelihood of injury. The symptoms of overtraining include listlessness, poor appetite, sleep disturbance and weight loss.

HOW CAN THE INCIDENCE OF INJURIES BE REDUCED?

The incidence of injuries can be reduced by:

- choosing a suitable programme or sport activity for the individual;
- ensuring that the individual is fit to participate;
- adopting appropriate safety and preventative measures;
- ensuring adequate supervision and good advice; and
- adhering to the rules of the chosen activity.

CHOICE OF PROGRAMME ACTIVITY

Any individual embarking on a new activity, or advising others, must take many factors into consideration when selecting an appropriate programme.

PHYSICAL CHARACTERISTICS

Participation in a sport or exercise for which an individual is not well suited may increase the likelihood of injury. Certain minor physical deformities (such as flat feet) would make an individual more prone to ankle, leg or knee injuries. An activity such as long distance road running would not therefore be advisable.

INTEREST

People take part in sport for different reasons - for the fun of it, to improve their skills, to compete against others, to win. Competitive sport can provide new challenges, increase enjoyment and may even become the prime motivation for continuing participation. Winners thrive on competition but striving for success can create psychological pressure, particularly if the competitive element is being encouraged by over-ambitious parents, teachers or coaches.

Exercise and sport should be fun and the needs and interests of the individual should always come first. Special consideration should be given to the interests of young people, women (especially expectant mothers), veterans and those with disabilities or special needs.

CHILDREN AND YOUNG PEOPLE

Children and young people are not mini-adults. They require specially designed programmes, not scaled-down adult sports or training plans. Steady, low-intensity exercise, with adequate periods of rest, is more suitable.

Although girls and boys are physically very similar before puberty, they have their peak growth rates at different ages - girls usually between 10 and 12, boys about two years later. During this growth period, their bones cannot cope with heavy or intensive training programmes. These could cause growing pains, affecting knees, heels, elbows, shoulders and the back. Specific strength and weight training should be avoided and strength developed naturally using their own body weight as a resistance (eg press-ups, pull-ups).

Providing children with good quality equipment can be expensive during this period of rapid growth and development. Growing children must be given the best quality footwear appropriate for their sport, even if this means a new pair of shoes every six to 12 months during a rapid growth spurt. The same principle applies to the use of protective equipment such as a mouth guard which should be individually fitted for the young person by their own dentist, and changed as often as necessary.

The physical changes at puberty may result in the need for changes in technique. Girls for example develop a wider pelvis (to facilitate child birth) and this may affect the running action and even cause pain in the front of the knee.

In addition to physical developments, childhood and adolescence may bring emotional stresses - particularly for early and late developers. It is important to ensure that young people enjoy sport and exercise programmes, that frustration is avoided by ensuring the activity is appropriate for them (emotionally as well as physically) and that competition is kept in perspective.

Girls may be sensitive about participating in sport when they start having periods and need reassurance that a normal period does not prevent participation in even the most vigorous activities.

WOMEN

Women may choose to regulate their periods by taking the contraceptive pill, but many find that they perform better at sport if they have a normal menstrual cycle.

Girls and women involved in very intense training programmes may find that their periods become scanty or even stop. If this occurs, the athlete should consult her doctor to check that there is nothing seriously wrong. In most cases, this condition will be corrected by adjusting the training programme, and gaining a little weight.

A normal pregnancy should not, as a rule, prevent physical activity, but it is important that pregnant women consult regularly with their general practitioner, or obstetrician, about the type and amount of exercise they are taking, adjusting their exercise programme as the pregnancy progresses. In the early months, brisk walking can help maintain fitness, but later, swimming is more appropriate. A good exercise programme throughout pregnancy will help maintain fitness and firm muscles, at the same time controlling unnecessary weight gain, and promoting the rapid return of a slim, active figure after the baby has been born.

Breast feeding does not rule out exercise, but a good supporting maternity bra is essential. It is important to choose the type of exercise carefully, as jogging would obviously be uncomfortable, whereas brisk walking, cycling and swimming would be beneficial.

VETERANS

Veterans (over the age of 40) need to follow sensible guidelines, particularly if they are just taking up or resuming sport at this age. A simple guide can be obtained by:

- consulting a doctor for a check on weight, pulse rate, blood pressure, heart, lungs, urine and blood;
- reassessing lifestyle, particularly with regard to the amount of

everyday exercise, dietary habits, drinking and smoking; and

- choosing an activity carefully, starting slowly and building up gradually; stretching exercises to maintain 'flexibility' are particularly important for veterans.

DISABLED PEOPLE

Disabled people and those with special needs benefit from appropriately selected active play, exercise or sport. Activity offers a healthier lifestyle, a feeling of well being and the opportunity for communication and contact with other people. It can be a challenge to find the right activity to suit individual physical or psychological capability. It is essential to consult a doctor before recommending or taking up any new activity.

The scope is wide, and advice is readily available from many organisations; see section 6.

FITNESS ASSESSMENT

If flexibility, strength, speed and endurance are inadequate for the chosen sport or activity, injuries are more likely to occur. It is important to know how to assess fitness as well as the type of fitness required for each sport.

General fitness can be gauged through health checks carried out by a doctor or less accurately through self-assessment measures (eg resting pulse rate, recovery time for return to resting rates following exercise). Athletes wishing to measure more accurately the components of fitness require either recognised field tests or a laboratory test. The latter is more costly and time consuming and should always be carried out by specialists at registered institutions[1]. Field tests are more accessible and sometimes more appropriate for the sport. Tests have been developed to measure endurance, strength, speed and flexibility and these can generally be carried out without specialist facilities. For example, the multi-stage fitness test[2] is a progressive shuttle run test which can be undertaken in a gym, on a field or a track. It will provide an estimation of endurance fitness.

Footnotes

1 For further information on laboratory and field fitness tests, contact the Sports Science Education Officer at the National Coaching Foundation, College Close, 4 Beckett Park, Leeds LS6 3QH

2 Available from the National Coaching Foundation.

FITNESS REQUIREMENTS

FLEXIBILITY

In all sports, some degree of flexibility (suppleness) is needed for effective performance and injury avoidance. Different muscles and tendons are at risk in different sports, and injuries will occur if a muscle is forced beyond its normal range of movement. Regular stretching improves the elasticity of muscles and tendons, and this should be carried out smoothly and under control by:

- slowly moving the muscle group concerned with a particular movement to the stretched position until discomfort (not pain) is felt; and

- holding the position for about ten to fifteen seconds.

"Never bounce when stretching".

Too much flexibility can also result in injury if there is insufficient strength to support the movement of the joint. It is equally important to maintain a balance in strength between groups of muscles that work against each other (eg between the hamstring muscles at the back of the thigh and the quadriceps at the front).

STRENGTH AND SPEED

Strength training should not be overdone and should be tailored to the needs of the individual. It is generally recommended that weights should not be used until bone development is complete (about 17 years). It should also be adapted to the activity in terms of the:

- muscles used (eg distance runners need less upper body strength work than gymnasts); and

- training load (eg the gymnast needs muscle strength gained by few repetitions of moving heavy loads, the runner needs muscle endurance gained by moving light loads with more frequent repetitions).

During injury, muscle wasting often occurs and it is important that muscle strength is regained before full training is resumed. Speed of movement is important to a number of sports and specific training is needed for its development.

ENDURANCE

Endurance is required to offset fatigue which usually results in the breakdown of skill - noticeable, for example, in the loss of style in the distance runner and the technique change in the tennis player. Performance is impaired and there is an increased risk of overuse injury.

Endurance fitness must be gained slowly if it is to be achieved safely and should be specific:

- cardio-respiratory fitness is gained by extending the body's ability to supply oxygen to the working muscle. Typically this involves exercising the large muscle groups (eg in running, swimming and cycling).

- local muscle endurance increases the stamina of a particular muscle group (eg sit-ups will increase the endurance of the stomach muscles but will contribute little to cardio-respiratory fitness).

SAFETY AND PREVENTATIVE MEASURES

WARM-UP

Warm-up is a very important factor in the prevention of injury. It should be used not just before the start but following any breaks in activity (eg after an interval, before each routine, race or bout). It should be enjoyable, related to the activity to follow and consist of three phases:

- full body exercises involving both arms and legs, carried out at a brisk pace (to raise body temperature and the rate of blood flow);

- slow, sustained stretching of each of the muscles, tendons and joints to prepare them for use, working systematically through the body and paying extra attention to those muscles likely to be placed under the greatest stress; and

- skill exercises to simulate the practice or competitive conditions to prepare mentally and physically.

COOL-DOWN

Cool-down is equally important at the end of the activity. This helps the body to recover gradually and prevents the build up of fluids in the muscles which can lead to subsequent soreness and stiffness. A cool-down, which might last about 15 minutes, should consist of mild, rhythmic activity and the gentle stretching of the muscles which have been working. Warm (not hot) baths, showers or massage may also help recovery.

SKILL

Injuries are more likely if technique is poor, if the skill level is inadequate for the situation (eg a highly skilled judo player should not compete against a novice) or where skills break down due to competitive stress or fatigue. More skilful performers are less prone to injury and less likely to cause injury.

Incorrect technique can result in overuse injuries so coaches must be able to assess and correct technique. Javelin throwers with poor technique are more likely to develop shoulder or elbow injuries (as well as a poorer throw).

A breaststroke swimmer with too wide a leg kick may suffer knee injuries (as well as a less efficient kick).

The acquisition of skill and good technique often takes many hours of repetitive practice which can result in overuse injuries. Skill development, like fitness, should be developed slowly and progressively.

CLOTHING, EQUIPMENT AND FACILITIES

Well designed clothing and good quality equipment are essential if accidents and injuries are to be avoided. Footwear design has advanced considerably and shoes must be appropriate to the individual, the sport and the surface. Participation in a range of sports will require more than one pair of shoes and if the feet are still growing, frequent replacement is essential although costly.

It is important that protective clothing is used for the purpose for which it has been designed. Lacrosse helmets protect the skull from frequent impacts, cycling helmets or riding hats from a single more serious impact. Protection may be impaired following a major impact or over a long period of time - even though no damage is apparent. Mouthguards should be used in contact sports and these must be made for the individual by a dentist. Individuals wearing glasses should use shatter-proof lenses or contact lenses, as a form of eye protection in squash.

Equipment should be of good quality and purpose built. Worn-out, part-serviceable or adapted equipment may cut costs but they frequently lead to accidents or injuries.

Sometimes equipment is used for a purpose for which it is not intended

or is adapted to meet a different need, eg judo mats being used for gymnastics. This is inappropriate and can result in injury.

Sport and exercise should always take place in a suitable and well-maintained environment. Obviously, an uneven or slippery surface, or a potholed football pitch, will increase the risk of injury. Protection should always be found against unavoidable hazards (eg fencing, posts, windows).

ADEQUATE SUPERVISION

Injuries in sport occur more frequently if there is inadequate supervision or poor control. This is particularly true in sports in which there is an element of danger (eg gymnastics, water sports, javelin), or where the conditions are cramped or skill level is low.

Many rules are designed to protect the safety of participants as well as to ensure fair play and an evenly balanced competition. These should always be enforced and those in charge should provide a good role model at all times. In addition, they should:

- be trained in First Aid;

- become appropriately trained in the activity (eg by the governing body of sport);

- plan the activities with safety in mind;

- maintain discipline;

- place themselves so that all participants are in view;

- use well-rehearsed safety calls (eg stop signals in a swimming pool);

- check the environment for hazards before and during the activity (eg lighting, surfaces, equipment);

- ensure that equipment is regularly checked and maintained; and

- ensure first aid equipment is readily available at all times.

Section 3

INJURIES

AND

ILLNESS

IN
SPORT

AIMS OF FIRST-AIDERS IN SPORT

The aims of first-aiders in sport are:

- to provide immediate care to minimise serious consequences of injury or illness;
- to promote recovery; and
- to encourage measures to prevent injury.

ACTION

- Use your head before your hands.

STAY COOL

- To "stay cool" and reassure an injured athlete, you need a basic knowledge of relevant First Aid which will help you adopt a systematic and reassuring approach to the injured athlete.

LOOK

- At the situation - is there any further danger?

LOOK

- At the patient - is he breathing normally, is his colour normal, is he conscious, is he bleeding, is the injured part obviously deformed?

LISTEN

- To the patient and to any witnesses. What happened?
- Is the patient talking and answering questions sensibly?

ASK

- The patient to try, very gently, to move the injured part(s) and demonstrate co-ordination (except when dealing with potentially serious neck injuries).

TOUCH

- Having used your head to get a good idea of what has happened to the patient, you can now use your hands to examine the injured part, comparing it to the other side of the body, head or limb.

IT IS IMPORTANT THAT NO FOOD OR DRINK IS GIVEN TO ANY INJURED PLAYER WHO MAY REQUIRE HOSPITAL TREATMENT.

BLEEDING

To operate efficiently the body has to have enough blood circulating at sufficient pressure to maintain delivery of nutriment and oxygen to all the body tissues. Severe blood loss in sport is unusual, but where it does occur, whether external or internal, it reduces the circulation and may result in the death of the casualty.

CHECKLIST FOR INITIAL ASSESSMENT

- Is the bleeding profuse? - Is the blood spurting? Flowing briskly? Are major blood vessels involved?

- Does the casualty show symptoms and signs of 'shock' - paleness, lightheadedness, nausea, cold, thirst?

ACTION

- Cover wound with clean pad if available and apply hand pressure. If pad is not available ask casualty to press on wound with his hand or fingers if he is capable of doing so. If not, use your hand to apply pressure to wound trying to keep edges of wound together. Wear disposable gloves, if available.

- Lay casualty down with head kept low.

- Raise bleeding part as high above the chest as possible.

- Apply sterile dressing and bandage firmly in position.

- Keep part raised and supported to prevent movement, and obtain medical assistance.

- If bleeding continues apply further pressure to dressing by padding and firmer bandage, or with your hand. Do not remove dressing already applied. Raise part further, if possible.

FOLLOW UP ADVICE

All wounds which have bled profusely should be seen by a doctor, as medical treatment is likely to be required to prevent later complications.

SHOCK

Shock is a condition in which the circulation fails because either the pressure or volume of circulating blood has fallen to a dangerous level and is insufficient to maintain normal function of the vital organs. The volume of blood in circulation may be reduced as a result of internal or external bleeding or burns. The blood pressure may also fall in sudden illness eg a heart attack. Other factors may result in a temporary reduction in blood pressure leading to a faint.

CHECKLIST FOR INITIAL ASSESSMENT

- Note colour of face, particularly areas normally pink in colour, eg inside of lips - have they become pale?

- Enquire for lightheadedness, nausea, cold or thirst.

- Observe the pulse and breathing. Rapid, weak pulse and shallow breathing with yawning or sighing are signs of shock.

- Feel the skin - cold clammy skin is a sign of shock.

ACTION

- Lay casualty down with head low, raise and support legs if possible.

- Loosen any tight clothing, particularly around chest and waist.

- Protect from cold, in particular put something under the casualty if he is on damp ground. If possible, transport to nearby shelter on a stretcher.

- Reassure with encouraging words.

- **DO NOT** give anything to drink or eat. The mouth may be moistened to help relieve thirst, but drinking or eating can be dangerous.

- If recovery is not rapid and complete, obtain medical help.

FOLLOW UP ADVICE

After recovery, strenuous exercise should be avoided for some time and activity built up gradually with medical approval.

UNCONSCIOUSNESS

Unconsciousness results from disturbance of the function of the brain. This may arise from head injury or from interference with the blood circulation to the brain. Reduction of blood flow to the brain may be temporary as in fainting, or more permanent as in heart attack or stroke. There are also other conditions which may affect the working of the brain, but irrespective of the cause of unconsciousness the casualty has three vital needs:

A an airway which is open and clear;

B adequate breathing; and

C sufficient circulation.

CHECKLIST FOR INITIAL ASSESSMENT

Is there a pulse? If so, speak to and touch casualty –

- is there any response?

Do his eyes open –

- spontaneously?
- on being spoken to?
- on painful stimulus?

Can he speak –

- normally?
- is he confused?

Does he move –

- spontaneously?
- on command?
- on painful stimulus?

ACTION

If no initial response:

- Open airway by tilting head back and supporting chin.
- Remove any obvious obstruction from mouth and throat.

Check breathing:

- If breathing present - place in Recovery Position.
- If not breathing, begin Artificial Ventilation **IMMEDIATELY** (see Resuscitation p56).
- Record levels of responsiveness periodically.
- Arrange urgent removal to hospital if recovery is not rapid and send record with casualty to hospital.

HEAD INJURY

Head injuries can result in damage to, or disturbance of, the brain. If this occurs, then concussion or compression may result and consciousness may be clouded or lost.

CONCUSSION

This is a condition of widespread but temporary disturbance of the brain sometimes described as "brain-shaking". It can result from a blow to the head, a fall from a height on to the feet or a blow on the point of the jaw.

In some cases unconsciousness may have been so brief that the casualty may be unaware of, or have forgotten, the initial incident. However, because concussion can precede brain compression, it is important to observe the casualty closely after any incident involving injury to the head.

The sporting participant should be advised to stop activity for assessment and possible medical advice.

COMPRESSION OF THE BRAIN

A serious condition produced by blood accumulating within the skull or by pressure from bone in a depressed fracture. Compression may develop at any time after apparent recovery from head injury.

CHECKLIST FOR INITIAL ASSESSMENT

Level of responsiveness - including assessment of eyes, speech and movement (see p18).

IF UNCONSCIOUS:

- Is casualty breathing?
- Is breathing noisy?

ACTION

IF UNCONSCIOUS:

- Tilt head backwards and lift chin, remove any obvious obstructions eg mouthguard, loose teeth.
- **CHECK BREATHING (LOOK, LISTEN AND FEEL)**
- If breathing adequate - place in recovery position (see p59).
- If not breathing commence resuscitation immediately (see p56).
- Arrange urgent removal to hospital.

IF CONSCIOUS:

- Check memory for recent events eg game score, and assess eyes, speech and movement (see p18).
- Enquire for symptoms of headache, nausea.
- For these less severe injuries with early apparent recovery, continue supervision and do not allow to drive or take alcohol.

CHECKLIST FOR ONGOING ASSESSMENT:

- Deterioration of level of responsiveness (see p18). Look for confusion, drowsiness, loss of co-ordination or fits.

- Headache and/or vomiting?

- Slow bounding pulse?

- Pupils unequal?

ACTION

- Arrange urgent removal to hospital.

FOLLOW UP ADVICE

Do not allow anyone with concussion or who has been knocked out, to participate in vigorous exercise or contact sport for two to four weeks, or combat sport for four to six weeks.

Anyone who is confused or knocked out for a second time within three months of their initial injury should then avoid contact or combat sport for a minimum of a further three months.

Anyone who has three concussions/ knockouts in a year should rest for a year or change to a non-contact sport.

After prolonged unconsciousness in hospital or brain surgery, sporting activity should only be resumed after medical advice.

FACIAL INJURIES

Individually made and fitted mouth guards should be worn in activities where there is danger of facial injury.

Injury to the face may be associated with damage to the brain or neck. The main danger is choking because the airway may become obstructed by displaced teeth, blood or saliva when the casualty is unable to swallow adequately to keep the airway clear.

CHECKLIST FOR INITIAL ASSESSMENT

- Is the casualty breathing satisfactorily?
- Is there bleeding from nose, mouth or skin?
- Is there difficulty in speaking or swallowing?
- Is there any deformity?
- Is there any disturbance of vision?

ACTION

- Clear the mouth of any loose material, dentures etc.
- Position casualty to ensure airway is kept clear:
  - Sitting - leaning forward.
  - Lying - in Recovery Position.
- Control bleeding and cover wounds.
- Obtain medical assistance.
- If teeth are partially dislocated but still attached to the gum margin, try gently to return them to the normal position. If a tooth has been knocked out and is intact with its root attached, ask the casualty to clean it by gently licking and sucking, then ask the casualty to place it in the mouth between cheek and gum. Arrange immediate dental care.

NOSE BLEEDING

- Sit the casualty with head well forward.
- Loosen any tight clothing around the neck and chest.
- Tell him to breathe through the mouth.
- Pinch nostrils firmly at soft part of nose for ten minutes (Fig 1.).
- Advise not to blow or pick nose for some time afterwards.
- If bleeding continues seek medical advice.

Note: Nose plugs should not be used.

Fig 1.

EYE INJURIES

Eye injuries are common in sport especially football, golf, squash and badminton. Inexperienced players and children are particularly vulnerable. Use of protective wide vision eye guards should be encouraged in squash.

CHECKLIST FOR INITIAL ASSESSMENT

- Do the circumstances indicate injury or a foreign body eg dirt or eyelash in the eye?

- Is there blood in or around the eye?

- Is there impairment of vision?

ACTION

- If the eye is injured, cover the closed eye with a clean dressing and remove casualty to hospital.

- Otherwise - a foreign body can be washed out with clean running water, or removed with a moistened swab or damp corner of a clean handkerchief.

- If a foreign body is under the upper eyelid, pull the upper eyelid gently downwards and outwards over the lower lid and allow lashes of lower lid to brush foreign body out.

DROWNING

Remember, anyone rescued from immersion in water[1] may be suffering as a result of cold, as well as the effects of inhaling water.

CHECKLIST FOR INITIAL ASSESSMENT

- Is the casualty conscious?

- If not conscious, is he breathing?

- Do the circumstances indicate possible injury eg diving in to shallow water?

- How cold is he?

ACTION

- If the casualty is unconscious and not obviously breathing, remove obvious obstructions from mouth and throat and begin Artificial Ventilation immediately - even before removing casualty from the water if possible.

- Remove casualty from water supporting head, neck and spine if there is a possibility of injury from diving or a fall. Lay casualty with head down slope if on a beach.

- Do not waste time trying to drain water from the lungs.

- Open the airway, check breathing, complete A, B & C of resuscitation as required.

- When breathing spontaneously, place casualty in recovery position even if not unconscious - he is liable to be sick.

- Remove wet clothing and dry casualty as early as possible, wrap in warm dry blankets, clothing etc. Treat hypothermia as appropriate.

- All casualties who may have inhaled water should be removed to hospital to ensure that there is no lung damage.

Footnotes

1   For further information contact the Royal Life Saving Society UK (see p83).

BENDS (Decompression Sickness)

After diving at length using self contained underwater breathing apparatus (SCUBA), rapid return to the surface may result in bubbles of nitrogen being formed in the tissues. This produces the symptoms and signs of decompression sickness.

CHECKLIST FOR INITIAL ASSESSMENT

- After a dive are there transient aches, itching or a rash?

- Is there pain at joints, resulting in incapacity?

- Is there any difficulty or pain in breathing?

- Is there any paralysis or loss of sensation?

ACTION

- Lay casualty down in recovery position and arrange urgent medical help.

- Removal to hospital or other centre. Decompression facilities will probably be required.

CHEST AND ABDOMINAL INJURIES

The chest and abdomen contain most of the body's vital organs. Injury to the chest may seriously interfere with breathing while damage to the abdomen may result in dangerous internal bleeding.

CHECKLIST FOR INITIAL ASSESSMENT

- Is the casualty able to breath adequately?
- Is breathing painful?
- Look at colour of face and condition of skin - is skin pale, cold, sweaty?
- Is there evidence of blood - coughed up, or passed in urine?
- Observe pulse and breathing at intervals - increasing rates indicate loss of blood from the circulation.
- Look for bruising and tenderness.
- Check front of abdomen for rigidity.

IMPORTANT

Some of these factors may take several hours to develop therefore act on suspicion if the circumstances of the incident indicate possibility of internal injury.

ACTION

- If casualty has difficult and/or painful breathing support him in a half sitting position, turned on to the injured side with the arm of that side supported in an elevation sling (Fig 2).

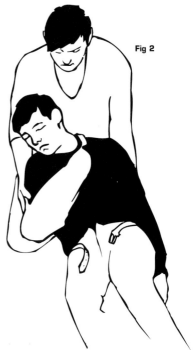

Fig 2

- Loosen clothing, particularly round the waist.
- If the casualty is pale and is breathing adequately, treat shock. Arrange removal to hospital.
- Do not give anything to eat or drink.
- Record pulse rates periodically and send this record with casualty to hospital.

WINDING

A blow in the pit of the stomach or having the chest crushed can cause a player to become winded. The player finds he cannot breathe in and lies gasping for breath. It is important not to interfere with players in these circumstances, allowing them to recover their own breath which usually takes approximately one minute. Loosen any tight clothing and you may consider lightly massaging the player's anterior abdominal wall. Do not pump the player up and down because this may cause further damage if there has been any internal injury.

INJURIES TO THE FEMALE BREAST

The breast can be damaged in either running or contact sport. It is important to ensure that women participating in sport wear an appropriate form of protective and supportive bra which does not damage the nipples.

Any bruise of the breast will always tend to settle in the lower half of the breast and may form a breast lump. It is important that any breast lump should be examined by a doctor irrespective of whether or not you may relate it to an injury.

TESTICULAR INJURIES

The testicles are suspended in a vulnerable position. A blow in the testicles is sickeningly painful. Usually the pain passes quite quickly, but if pain persists a doctor should be consulted as soon as possible. If a player develops pain in a testicle while training or playing without sustaining an injury he should see a doctor as soon as possible.

SOFT TISSUE INJURIES

CUTS AND GRAZES

CHECKLIST FOR INITIAL ASSESSMENT

- Is blood flowing from the wound?
- Is there dirt in or around the wound?
- Is there any associated loss of function?

ACTION

- Control bleeding (see p19).
- If bleeding is not severe:
  - If possible wash your hands before treating the wound, and wear disposable gloves if available.
  - Wash wound thoroughly with running water if available:
    - Keeping the wound covered, clean area around wound with soap and water. Use clean material (ie gauze) and dispose of it safely. Dab gently to dry.
    - Cover area with suitable dressing and secure in position.
    - Wash your hands as soon as possible after treating wound.

FOLLOW UP ADVICE

If tetanus immunisation is not up to date suggest that this is now done. If you have not been able to clean wound thoroughly seek medical advice. Increasing pain in the wound or swelling and redness developing later may indicate infection of the wound.

- Advise casualty to seek medical aid should this occur.
- Get a Tetanus booster every five years.

BRUISES

CHECKLIST FOR INITIAL ASSESSMENT

- Has the force applied been sufficient to cause internal injury?

- Is there any loss of function of the part?

- Is there any tenderness on bone in the area?

- Are there symptoms or signs of shock? (see p20).

ACTION

- If the answer is 'yes' to any of the above questions, suspect more serious injury and treat appropriately.

- If in doubt about severity of injury seek medical advice.

- Otherwise - raise and support part in comfortable position.

- Apply ice pack or cold compresses.

FOLLOW UP ADVICE

If pain persists or any disability develops, seek medical advice.

INJURIES TO MUSCLES, LIGAMENTS AND TENDONS

Muscles consist of thousands of fibres bound together within a sheath of connective tissue.

When the muscle fibres are **overstretched** or torn a "**strain**" results.

Tendons are cords of tissue which connect muscle to bone, to enable muscles to move bones at joints. These tendons may become inflamed - Tendonitis - or torn eg rupture of Achilles Tendon. Some tendons pass through a sheath which is lined with synovial membrane, which can become inflamed (tenosynovitis).

Ligaments are made up of fibrous tissue which hold bones together at joints; these ligaments may be overstretched or torn, eg by wrenching of a joint, resulting in a "**sprain**".

CHECKLIST FOR INITIAL ASSESSMENT

- How did the injury occur? - Were the forces involved severe?

- Is there significant loss of function of the part?

- Is there tenderness over the bone in the area?

- Is there any deformity of the part?

- Are there symptoms and signs of shock (see Shock p20).

ACTION

- If the answer to any of these questions is 'yes', suspect more serious injury – treat as fracture (see p33).

- If in doubt seek medical advice.

- Otherwise – rest and support the part in the most comfortable position.

- Ice pack or cold compresses should be applied to the part.

- Compression bandaging will help limit swelling and subsequent disability.

- Elevate the part to limit the blood flow to the injured area and reduce swelling by promoting drainage by gravity.

FOLLOW UP ADVICE

Keep the part rested for 24 to 72 hours before gently exercising within the limits of pain, gradually increasing the exercise daily until full fitness is restored. If pain persists or disability develops, seek medical advice.

INJURIES TO BONES AND JOINTS

Even if moderate force is applied to the bones and joints of the body, bones can be cracked or broken – **fracture** – or, bones can be displaced at a joint – **dislocation**.

CHECKLIST FOR INITIAL ASSESSMENT

- Did the casualty feel or hear a 'snap'?
- Is there difficulty in moving the part normally?
- Is there any tenderness over a bone or joint?
- Is there deformity of the part?
- Are there symptoms and signs of shock?
- Is there a wound associated with the site of injury?

ACTION

- If the answer is 'yes' to any of these questions, assume a significant injury.

- Steady and support the injured part in the position found.

- Cover any wound with a suitable dressing.

- Do not attempt to replace dislocated joint to normal position.

- Immobilise the part by "splintage" to a sound part of the casualty's body (see p64).

- Treat shock (see p20).

- Have casualty removed to hospital.

SPINAL INJURY

The spine is made up of a column of bones called vertebrae, which are separated by discs which act as shock absorbers. The spinal column is held together by ligaments, and is supported by the muscles of the trunk.

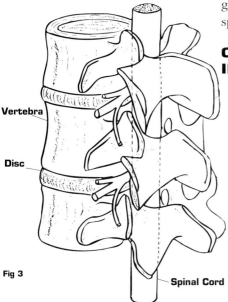

Vertebra

Disc

Fig 3

Spinal Cord

The spinal cord from the brain passes through a canal formed by the vertebrae (Fig 3.). It is a very delicate structure and if damaged can result in loss or disturbance of power or sensation in all parts of the body below the injured area. This may be temporary, but will be permanent if the cord is partially or completely severed.

Therefore the greatest care must be taken in dealing with a neck or back injury when fracture is suspected.

The two most vulnerable areas of the spinal column are the neck and lower back. In sport the most common activities in which spinal injuries occur are diving, swimming, rugby football, gymnastics, horse riding and motor sport.

CHECKLIST FOR INITIAL ASSESSMENT

● Do circumstances of the accident suggest possibility of spinal injury?

● Establish site and severity of pain.

● Ask to move wrists/ankles; fingers/toes - movement may be weak.

● Test sensation by gently touching limbs below site of injury.

● Ask if tingling/numb sensation.

Remember, spinal injury is not excluded by absence of above signs, any disturbance of feeling or movement however slight or however temporary, should raise the possibility of a spinal fracture or spinal cord injury.

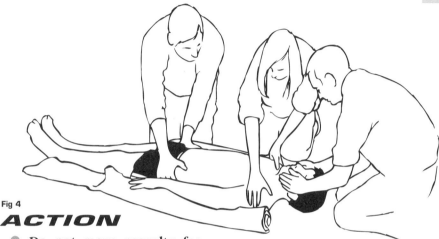

Fig 4

ACTION

- **Do not move casualty for reasons of convenience - wait for expert help or ambulance to arrive.**

- **Reassure casualty and tell not to move.**

- **Maintain position in which found unless danger or priority of airway, breathing or circulation dictate otherwise.**

- Steady and support head and neck in neutral position by placing your hands over casualty's ears. Get bystanders to support shoulders and hips.(Fig 4).

- Clothing or rolled blankets alongside will give added support.

- Cover with blanket to minimise shock.

- If fracture suspected in neck - loosen clothing at casualty's neck and apply a neck collar for added stability.

- Support of head and neck must be maintained by hands until arrival at hospital.

- If vomiting likely to occur, place casualty in the SPINAL INJURY RECOVERY POSITION (see p61).

- If movement of the casualty is imperative use plenty of helpers to ensure the spine is moved in 'one piece'.

If the casualty is unconscious and spinal injury suspected:

- Check breathing; if casualty not breathing – open airway by jaw lift, and if this is unsuccessful - slight head tilt. Give mouth to mouth ventilation if necessary.

- Check circulation and give external chest compression if necessary.

- If breathing, place in Spinal Injury Recovery Position and carry out treatment as above as far as possible.

SHOULDER AND UPPER LIMB

The shoulder girdle and upper limbs consist of the shoulder blade (scapula), the collar bone (clavicle), the upper arm (humerus), forearm (radius and ulna), the wrist and the hand. They are covered with powerful muscles.

There are two joints in the region of the shoulder - the shoulder joint itself and the small joint between the collar bone and the shoulder blade (acromio-clavicular) which lies on top of the shoulder joint.

The stability of the shoulder joint depends on the cuff of muscles attached to the top of the humerus (the rotator cuff). The muscles and tendons around the shoulder joint are commonly strained and should receive basic soft tissue injury treatment. Medical advice may also be required.

FRACTURE OF THE COLLAR BONE (CLAVICLE)

This usually results from a fall on to the point of the shoulder or more rarely the elbow or outstretched hand. It is the most common of all fractures and occurs at all ages.

CHECKLIST FOR INITIAL ASSESSMENT

- Checklist as for bone and joint injuries (see p33).
- Does casualty support the arm of injured side with head inclined towards it?

ACTION

- Support and immobilise the upper limb (see p64).
- Remove casualty to hospital.

ACROMIO-CLAVICULAR JOINT INJURY

This joint is usually injured by a fall on to the top of the shoulder. It may simply be sprained with pain and little or no swelling, or be subluxed (partialy dislocated) or dislocated with a visible swelling or step-like deformity. This injury is common in young adults, especially in rugby and wrestling.

CHECKLIST FOR INITIAL ASSESSMENT

- Checklist as for bone and joint injuries (see p33).
- Is there deformity as described above?

ACTION

- Support and immobilise the upper limb.
- Apply an ice pack.
- Remove casualty to hospital.

FOLLOW UP ADVICE

Following a sprain, if pain increases or progress is slow, seek medical advice.

DISLOCATED SHOULDER

A dislocation of the shoulder joint is caused by a fall on the outstretched hand, elbow or the point of the shoulder. Typically the shoulder will lose its normal round appearance and take on a more square shape (Fig 5).

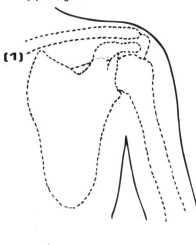

Fig 5 (1) Undamaged Shoulder;
     (2) Damaged Shoulder

(1)

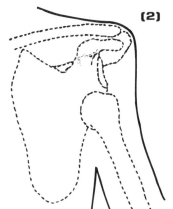

(2)

In a few instances, dislocation may be associated with damage to nerves giving tingling or numbness in the arm and hand.

Some patients suffer with recurrent dislocation of the shoulder; in such cases the joint can dislocate with relatively little force. Most of these patients eventually need surgery which leaves them with a slight restriction of movement.

CHECKLIST FOR INITIAL ASSESSMENT

● Is the typical deformity present?

ACTION

● Support the arm in an arm sling.
● Remove the casualty to hospital without delay.

FRACTURE OF THE UPPER ARM BONE (HUMERUS)

This fracture results from a direct blow, a fall on to the arm or from the arm being twisted or bent.

CHECKLIST FOR INITIAL ASSESSMENT

- Checklist as for bone and joint injuries (see p33).

ACTION

- Support and immobilise the injured limb (see p64).

- Remove casualty to hospital.

DISLOCATION OF THE ELBOW

This injury is caused by falling on to the outstretched hand. The forearm is driven backwards on the upper arm making the tip of the elbow more prominent. This may also produce nerve injury with tingling or numbness in the fingers and hand, or interference with circulation to the hand.

CHECKLIST FOR INITIAL ASSESSMENT

- Is the above deformity present?

- Is the pulse present at the wrist?

ACTION

- Support the arm comfortably, use an arm sling if the elbow is bent.

- Remove the casualty to hospital without delay.

'TENNIS' AND 'GOLFERS' ELBOW

Pain on the outside of the elbow occurs in the condition known as "tennis" elbow. It is an over-use injury which is not only produced in racquet sports but can occur with any repetitive movement. It is best treated by rest for a few days, ice packs, mild pain relieving tablets and supporting bandage to the muscles of the forearm.

If the symptoms do not settle in a few days seek medical advice. Try to identify the cause of the problem such as an inappropriate technique or equipment.

"Golfer's" elbow affects the inside of the elbow and the cause and treatment are similar to "Tennis" elbow.

FRACTURE OF FOREARM AND WRIST

FRACTURE OF THE FOREARM AND WRIST

This is caused in a similar manner to fractures of the humerus.

CHECKLIST FOR INITIAL ASSESSMENT

● Checklist as for the bone and joint injuries (see p33).

ACTION

● Support and immobilise the injured part (see p64).

● Remove the casualty to hospital.

SPRAINS OF THE THUMB

The ligaments at the base of the thumb are frequently injured in sport when the thumb is caught and twisted or bent. If completely torn these ligaments usually require surgical repair. A complete tear should be suspected if there is severe swelling or if bruising appears.

CHECKLIST FOR INITIAL ASSESSMENT

- Is the swelling severe?
- Is there any bruising?

ACTION

- If the answers are "no", then treat as ligament sprain (see p32).
- If any answer is "yes", apply a supporting bandage and an elevation sling and seek medical advice.

SPRAINS OF THE FINGER JOINTS

SPRAINS OF THE FINGER JOINTS

These joints are frequently injured in sports, particularly involving hand contact. If the joint moves abnormally (from side to side) the ligament is completely torn.

CHECKLIST FOR INITIAL ASSESSMENT

- Is there abnormal movement?

ACTION

- If the answer is "yes", seek medical advice.
- If the answer is "no", tape lightly to adjoining fingers ("buddy" strapping) while still allowing movement of the finger joint.

FOLLOW UP ADVICE

Spindle shaped swelling and discomfort may persist for several months. When participating in sport over the next few months protect the injured finger by re-applying "buddy" strapping.

DISLOCATION OF THE FINGERS

If twisting or bending force is severe, dislocation of finger joints may occur. There is an obvious step-shaped deformity of the affected joint.

CHECKLIST FOR INITIAL ASSESSMENT

● Is deformity present?

ACTION

● A firm steady pull on the displaced part along the line of the finger usually allows the dislocation to slip back into place. This may be attempted once. If successful assess and treat as for sprains of the finger. If unsuccessful remove casualty to hospital.

MALLET FINGER

'MALLET' FINGER

A sharp blow on the top of the finger whilst it is straight eg from a ball, may force forward the joint at the end of the finger. This can damage or tear the tendon which holds the finger straight and this joint droops.

CHECKLIST FOR INITIAL ASSESSMENT

● Is deformity present?
● Is the casualty unable to straighten the finger tip?

ACTION

● Seek medical advice.

PELVIC GIRDLE AND LOWER LIMB INJURIES

Each lower limb consists of the thigh bone (femur), the leg bones (tibia and fibula) and the bones at the ankle and foot. The kneecap (patella) is a bone which lies within the large tendon on the front of the knee which straightens the knee.

The femur is joined to the pelvic girdle at the hip joint which is a very stable ball and socket joint and covered by many muscles.

The knee joint is a shallow joint, deepened on each side by a cartilage (meniscus) and is entirely supported by ligaments and tendons.

The ankle joint is shaped like a mortice joint and is moderately stable, but it is supported on either side by ligaments and tendons. Many bones make up the arches of the foot. They are small and entirely supported by ligaments and tendons. For this reason the foot requires to be supported in good quality footwear appropriate to the sporting activity.

DISLOCATION OF THE HIP

This is an uncommon injury in sport but may occur if the leg is driven backwards on the pelvis. There is usually extreme pain in the hip and the leg characteristically lies bent forwards at the hip, turned inwards and tending to lie over the other leg.

CHECKLIST FOR INITIAL ASSESSMENT

- Is the characteristic deformity present?

ACTION

- Do not attempt to straighten or splint the leg.
- Support the limb comfortably in the position found.
- Arrange removal to hospital without delay.

GROIN STRAIN

Groin strain is a complex problem arising in sport and has many different causes. It usually involves inflammation or strain of the tendons of the thigh or abdomen where they are attached to the bones of the pelvis or the femur.

Groin strain is a chronic problem, best treated by rest with advice from a chartered physiotherapist or doctor. The cause of the condition must be identified and eliminated from the affected person's exercise pattern.

FRACTURE OF THE THIGH OR LEG

FRACTURE OF THE THIGH OR LEG

These fractures result from a violent injury.

CHECKLIST FOR INITIAL ASSESSMENT

- Checklist as for bone and joint injuries (see p33).

ACTION

- Handle the limb gently with adequate support.
- Apply an appropriate dressing to any wound.
- Immobilise the injured limb (see p67).
- Arrange removal to hospital without delay.

INJURIES OF THE KNEE

PAIN IN THE KNEECAP

Also known as 'anterior knee pain', 'patello-femoral pain' and 'chondromalacia patellae'.

The condition results from abnormal rubbing of the back of the kneecap on the lower end of the thighbone (femur) due to a combination of factors including imbalanced pull of the muscles at the front of the knee. It is most common in runners and jumpers, especially in women which may be due to certain anatomical differences in the shape of their pelvis.

Pain is experienced behind the kneecap often associated with a creaking noise which occurs during or after exercise or going up and down stairs. The acute pain can be relieved by the application of an ice pack and taking mild pain relieving tablets. However, prevention requires a carefully balanced muscle training programme to build up the muscle on the inner aspect at the front of the lower thigh. This is best supervised by a chartered physiotherapist.

LIGAMENT INJURIES

There is a large ligament on each side of the knee (collateral ligaments) and two within the knee joint (cruciate ligaments) (Fig 6.).

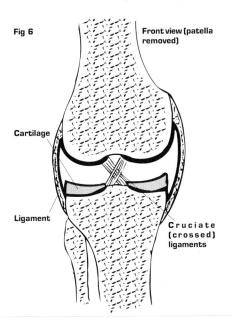

Fig 6

Front view (patella removed)

Cartilage

Ligament

Cruciate (crossed) ligaments

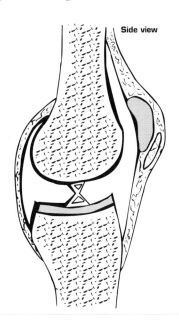

Side view

The collateral ligaments are injured by any force which pushes or twists the knee on either side in an abnormal direction.

This injury may be a simple sprain which requires treatment by the basic principles used to treat soft tissues injuries (see p30). A more severe force will rupture the ligament completely and allow abnormal side to side movement at the knee. It most commonly affects the inner (medial) ligament and requires hospital treatment. Cruciate ligament injuries occur as a complication of the severe collateral ligament injury described above, or following a direct blow to the front of the shin, or knee. A cruciate ligament injury requires hospital treatment.

CHECKLIST FOR INITIAL ASSESSMENT

- How did the injury occur?
- Is there obvious swelling in the knee joint soon after the injury?
- Is there abnormal side to side, or back and forward movement?

ACTION

- If either abnormality is present, support the knee in the most comfortable position and remove the casualty to hospital without delay.

TORN CARTILAGE (MENISCUS)

There are two half moon shaped cartilages in the knee, one on either side, which act as shock absorbers. They may be torn if the bent leg is violently twisted at the knee while bearing weight. This may cause the knee to "lock" or give way. It is an extremely common injury in football and may be associated with damage to the corresponding collateral ligament as described above.

CHECKLIST FOR INITIAL ASSESSMENT

- How did the injury occur?
- Is complete straightening or bending of the knee restricted?
- Is the pain and tenderness mainly on one side of the knee?

ACTION

- If either abnormality is present, apply a supporting bandage and seek medical advice.

Note: A good guide as to the severity of a joint injury is how quickly the joint swells after the injury. A rapid development of swelling (within 10-30 minutes, may be due to bleeding in the cavity of the joint and is called a "Haemarthrosis". Slow development of swelling (over several hours) is due to an accumulation of synovial fluid from the synovial membrane, and is known as a "synovial effusion". Bleeding in the joint is a severe injury and should be referred directly to hospital.

KNEE PAIN IN CHILDREN

KNEE PAIN IN CHILDREN

In addition to any of the above conditions, children can develop pain and swelling localised to the normal prominence on the front of the upper shin just below the kneecap during and after activity. It is due to the large tendon at the front of the knee pulling on the growing part of the bone. It will settle completely once the child is fully grown, but during the painful period symptoms can be controlled by reduction in exercise.

CHECKLIST FOR INITIAL ASSESSMENT

- Pain over the upper shin on activity?
- Is there swelling and tenderness where the tendon joins the upper shin?

ACTION

- Reduce activities.
- If the symptoms are severe or do not settle, seek medical advice?
- Increasing pain and swelling in a child's knee should always be investigated by an orthopaedic surgeon.

'SHIN SPLINTS'

Many middle distance runners experience pain in the front of the leg which is known as "shin splints". The pain can be due to several different causes including inflammation of the muscles and tendons attached to the shin, or to a stress fracture of the leg bone (tibia or fibula). Any athlete presenting with soft tissue "shin splints" should reduce the training programme, run on a soft surface such as grass and check that the quality of shoes is appropriate to the workload undertaken. However, stress fractures need a few weeks to heal, and are likely to be aggravated by continued running; walking should do no harm though.

If these measures do not ease the symptoms, seek appropriate medical advice.

ACUTE COMPARTMENT COMPRESSION SYNDROME

ACUTE COMPARTMENT COMPRESSION SYNDROME

Very occasionally a sportsman can complain of lower leg pain associated with a feeling of numbness and weakness in the foot. This is due to swelling of the muscles impairing circulation. It may manifest as a form of '**shin splints**'.

CHECKLIST FOR INITIAL ASSESSMENT

- Is the pain increased by movement of the toes or foot?
- Does the pain last for a few minutes after stopping the activity which caused it?

ACTION

- Make an appointment to see a consultant specialising in Sports medicine. If the pain is severe and the patient has ACUTE CCS he should be taken directly to hospital.

ACHILLES TENDON INJURIES

The achilles tendon joins the calf muscles to the heel and works vigorously lifting the body weight upwards and forwards during walking or running. The tendon may rupture during activity and this is often described as feeling like a "kick on the back of the ankle".

A more common and very complex problem, especially in runners, is inflammation and degeneration in the tendon itself, (tendonitis) or the fine sheath around the tendon (paratendonitis) which is aggravated by exercise.

ACHILLES TENDONITIS

CHECKLIST FOR INITIAL ASSESSMENT

- Is there swelling of the tendon?
- Is there tenderness of the tendon?

ACTION

- If acute, treat as tendon injury (see p32).
- If chronic, reduce activity and run on soft surfaces, check on sports footwear.
- If no improvement, seek medical advice.

RUPTURE OF ACHILLES TENDON

RUPTURE OF ACHILLES TENDON

CHECKLIST FOR INITIAL ASSESSMENT

- How did the injury occur?
- Is there a gap which can be felt in the tendon?
- Can the toe and the foot be actively pointed downwards?

ACTION

- If suspicious, remove casualty to hospital.

ANKLE INJURIES

Twisting injuries of the ankle are common in all sports, (affecting also spectators) and frequently result in damage to the ligaments on either side of the ankle.

Most injuries, particularly those affecting the outside of the joint, are sprains. (Fig 7).

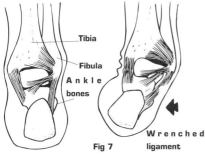

Fig 7

Tibia

Fibula

Ankle bones

Wrenched ligament

A severe twisting injury of the ankle can result in fracture of the bones.

CHECKLIST FOR INITIAL ASSESSMENT

● Is the patient unable to walk?

● Is there a great deal of swelling?

● Are there signs to suggest a fracture?

ACTION

● If the answer to any of the above is "yes", immobilise the limb (see p67) and seek medical advice.

● If the answer to all the above is "no", treat as a minor sprain (see p32).

Anyone with a minor sprain should be encouraged to walk in a normal fashion. It is better to walk slowly with a normal heel to toe gait, putting the ankle through as full a range of movement as possible. This will reduce strain injuries higher in the leg.

FOLLOW UP ADVICE

During recovery, attention should be paid to exercises which strengthen the leg muscles, restore full range of movement and improve balance and coordination. This will minimise the limp and help to avoid recurrent injuries of the ankle.

FOOT PROBLEMS

Pain in the foot is frequently related to strain of the ligaments supporting the bones which make up the arch of the foot. The pain is aggravated by inappropriate footwear with insufficient arch support.

Any sports person presenting with foot problems should reduce the training programme, run on a soft surface such as grass and check that the footwear gives adequate arch support.

If the problem continues, refer to a specialist.

COLD EXPOSURE

HYPOTHERMIA

Hypothermia develops when the body temperature falls from the normal 37°C to below 35°C. This condition is caused when taking part in an activity in chilling conditions eg cold, wet windy weather, or immersion in cold water, and is aggravated by drinking alcohol. Hypothermia can occur particularly in unfit individuals when they become tired and slow down.

To minimise the risk of suffering from hypothermia, plan and train for the activity, recognising the possibility of adverse weather conditions and having due regard to the capabilities of the participants. Wear appropriate clothing, several layers of loose clothing with an outer waterproof layer providing the best protection. Carry spare dry clothing, a survival bag and take high energy foods.

CHECKLIST FOR INITIAL ASSESSMENT

- Does the casualty feel cold to touch and is he shivering?
- Is the casualty forgetful confused, clumsy eg stumbling, or short tempered?

Note:

When core temperature drops below about 33°C, shivering stops.

ACTION

- Do not continue activity which has caused hypothermia.

- Provide shelter from cooling conditions.

- If possible, remove wet clothing and replace with dry clothing.

- It is important that casualty should be kept dry and insulated from cold and dampness, including the ground, using sleeping bag, blankets or survival bag.

- If possible, give hot drinks and high energy foods if conscious and able to swallow.

- Individuals unaffected by the conditions should be sent for help to evacuate casualty by stretcher.

FROSTBITE

This is a condition where extreme cold causes tissue damage in the extremities eg in fingers, toes, ears, nose and cheeks.

To minimise the risk of frostbite, wear adequate boots, mittens and cover the skin of the face as much as possible.

CHECKLIST FOR INITIAL ASSESSMENT

- Has the casualty been exposed to freezing temperatures?

- Has the casualty complained of tingling and pain followed by numbness?

- Is the affected area pale, mottled blue or black in colour?

ACTION

- Handle the affected part gently.

- Warm the affected area slowly and naturally with continuing protection against cold.

- Arrange removal to hospital.

EFFECTS OF OVERHEATING

Heat Exhaustion and Heatstroke are caused by failure to maintain body temperature by adequate sweating during exercise in hot, humid conditions. However, they might occur for no obvious reason in temperate conditions. They may also be made worse by vomiting or diarrhoea and occur in endurance events particularly in competitors who are unwell at the start.

HEAT EXHAUSTION

This condition is caused by failure to maintain an adequate intake of fluid or to replace lost fluid and salt from the body when undertaking activities in hot humid conditions.

CHECKLIST FOR INITIAL ASSESSMENT

- Are prevailing conditions likely to lead to heat exhaustion?

- Is the casualty feeling sick, thirsty, lightheaded?

- Is the casualty sweating?

- Are there muscular cramps?

ACTION

- Lay casualty down in cool shade.

- If conscious and able to swallow give water or flavoured squashes to drink to which about 0.5 teaspoonful of salt per 0.5 litre (1 pint) has been added.

- If symptoms persist seek medical advice.

FOLLOW UP ADVICE

- Rest and drink plenty of fluids.

- Do not undertake strenuous activity for at least two hours.

HEATSTROKE

If in hot conditions, or in certain illnesses, the body cannot control its temperature by sweating, the body temperature will rise, and confusion, convulsions and unconsciousness may develop.

Heatstroke is where the body temperature is raised above 37°C and persists at this level for some time after exercise. Rectal temperature above 40°C more than 10 minutes after exercise needs urgent treatment or it may lead to brain damage and so called heatstroke in which the subject becomes confused and may have convulsions. If the temperature is over 40°C start tepid sponging, fan, and if a doctor is available, give intravenous fluids. If the temperature does not fall arrange rapid transfer to hospital and sponge and fan on route.

CHECKLIST FOR INITIAL ASSESSMENT

- Are prevailing conditions likely to lead to heatstroke?
- Is the casualty hot and flushed?
- Is the casualty confused?

ACTION

- If unconscious, open airway, check breathing. Requires urgent treatment, resuscitate if necessary and place in recovery position.

- Remove to cool shade.
- Remove clothing, wet skin with cool water and fan with towel etc to reduce body temperature.
- If conscious and able to swallow give water or flavoured squashes to drink, to which about 0.5 teaspoonful of salt per 0.5 litre (1 pint) has been added.
- Remove to hospital.

IMPORTANT:

Anyone who collapses in an endurance event should have a rectal temperature taken if possible.

Note:

ACCLIMATISATION

The effects of overheating may be precipitated by inadequate acclimatisation. Depending on such factors as the distance travelled, the resultant fatigue, temperature and humidity, and altitude, a sportsperson may need several days to acclimatise before being ready to compete. Training has to be very carefully controlled, especially during the first few days.

Section 4

PRACTICAL

PROCEDURES

THE A.B.C. OF RESUSCITATION

AIRWAY

- In all unconscious casualties, a clear airway to the lungs is essential.
- Open the airway by tilting the head back and lifting the chin forward.
- Remove any obvious obstruction to breathing.

BREATHING

- Check if the casualty is breathing.
- Put your ear close to the casualty's mouth and nose, look at the chest (Fig 8.).

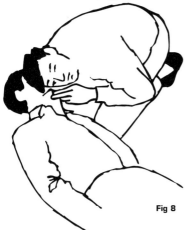

Fig 8

LISTEN, FEEL and **LOOK** for breathing.

- If you do not detect breathing **BEGIN ARTIFICIAL VENTILATION IMMEDIATELY**.

- Keep the airway open by tilting the head back and supporting the chin.
- Seal the nose by pinching the nostrils.
- Take a deep breath, open your mouth and, covering the casualty's mouth with yours, breathe into his mouth (Fig 9.).

Fig 9

Adequate inflation will cause the chest to rise.

- Raise your head from the casualty to allow him to breathe out, while you take another deep breath.
- If you are unable to inflate the casualty's lungs - check position of the casualty's head and try again.
- Give two full ventilations.

CIRCULATION

- After two full breaths, check the casualty's pulse in the neck:
  - Place two fingers on the voice box, slide them towards you into the hollow between the windpipe and the muscles at the side of the neck (Fig 10.).

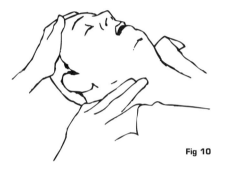

Fig 10

- If a pulse is detected, continue Artificial Ventilation until natural breathing is restored.
- If no pulse is felt **begin** External Chest Compression:
  - Locate the lower rib margin where it meets the soft abdominal wall.
  - Run your fingers along the rib margin to locate the lower end of the breastbone.
  - Measure two finger breadths about this point and place the heel of your hand along the line of the breastbone (Fig 11.).

- Place your other hand on top of the first, interlocking your fingers to keep them off the rib cage.

- With your elbows straight and your shoulders directly over your hands press the breastbone downwards 4 to 5 cms (1.5 to 2 ins) on an adult. Release the pressure without removing your hands from the chest. Repeat at a rate of 80 per minute.

- After 15 compressions ventilate the lungs twice.

- Repeat cycles of 15 compressions and two ventilations.

- Check pulse in the neck after one minute (four cycles) and thereafter at three minute intervals. When a pulse has returned stop the chest compressions and continue Artificial Ventilation until natural breathing is restored, then place casualty in Recovery Position (see p59).

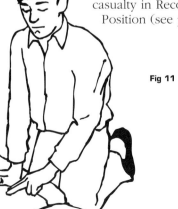

Fig 11

IMPORTANT

No harm will be done to the casualty if Artificial Ventilation is given and the casualty is still breathing, but External Chest Compression is dangerous if performed when the heart is beating even feebly. Therefore External Chest Compression must not be given unless the signs of failure of circulation are positively identified ie:

- The casualty is unconscious
- There is no breathing
- There is no pulse in the neck after ventilating the lungs twice

When performing External Chest Compression the casualty must be on a firm surface. The pressure must be by the heel of the hand only and directed to the breastbone only – not onto the front of the ribs.

Excessive pressure will cause internal injury, so the pressure must be appropriately reduced for small adults, children and infants.

RECOVERY POSITION

The Recovery Position is used for the unconscious casualty who is breathing, or where in a conscious casualty there is a risk of airway obstruction due to vomiting or injury.

- Kneel facing across the casualty's chest.

- Turn casualty's head towards you.

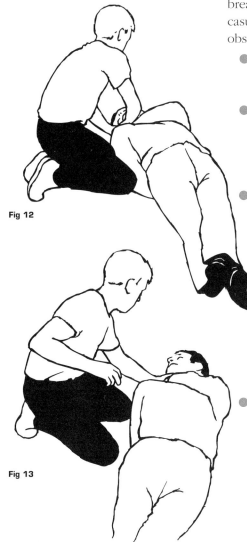

Fig 12

- Place his nearer arm close to his trunk with the hand under the hip, cross his far leg over the nearer one and bring his front arm across his chest towards you (Fig 12.).

- Protect the head with one hand (Fig 13.).

  /continued...

Fig 13

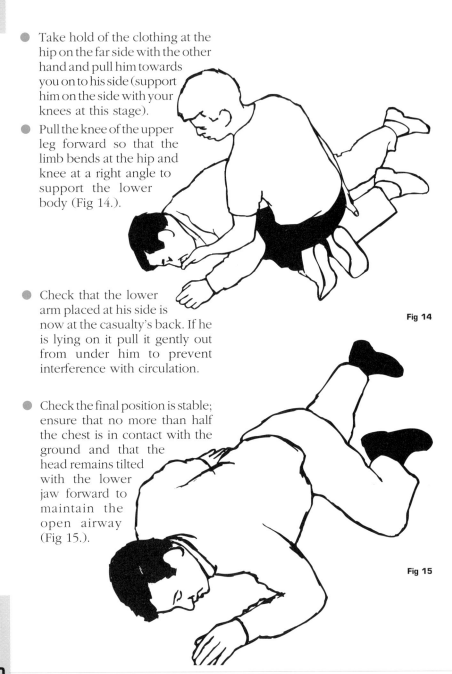

- Take hold of the clothing at the hip on the far side with the other hand and pull him towards you on to his side (support him on the side with your knees at this stage).

- Pull the knee of the upper leg forward so that the limb bends at the hip and knee at a right angle to support the lower body (Fig 14.).

- Check that the lower arm placed at his side is now at the casualty's back. If he is lying on it pull it gently out from under him to prevent interference with circulation.

Fig 14

- Check the final position is stable; ensure that no more than half the chest is in contact with the ground and that the head remains tilted with the lower jaw forward to maintain the open airway (Fig 15.).

Fig 15

SPINAL INJURY RECOVERY POSITION

If a spinal injury is suspected in the unconscious casualty the greatest care must be taken to place the casualty in the Spinal Injury Recovery Position without twisting or bending the spine. Ideally, six people should be used if the casualty has to be turned, using the "Log Roll" technique. As a first requirement the head should be supported in the normal neutral position (nose, navel and toes in line). Once established, this support should be maintained until the casualty arrives in hospital. All movement should be co-ordinated by the person supporting the casualty's head.

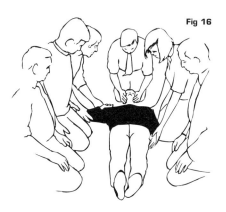

Fig 16

LOG ROLL TECHNIQUE

- Three helpers kneel along one side of the trunk, with two on the other side.
- Straighten the casualty's legs.
- Bend the elbow of the arm on the side of the three helpers and place the hand alongside the head. Place the other arm by his side (Fig 16.).
- The three helpers place their arms over the casualty and gently roll him on to his side with the other two helpers assisting to achieve this position while the head is being supported in the normal neutral position.

- Place the bent lowermost arm under the head to assist support of the head.
- Stabilise the trunk by bending the uppermost leg to a right angle at the hip (Fig 17.).

Fig 17

SLINGS

TRIANGULAR BANDAGE

The triangular bandage has a Point – the right angled corner ; Ends – the other corners and a Base – the longest border (Fig 18.).

Fig 18

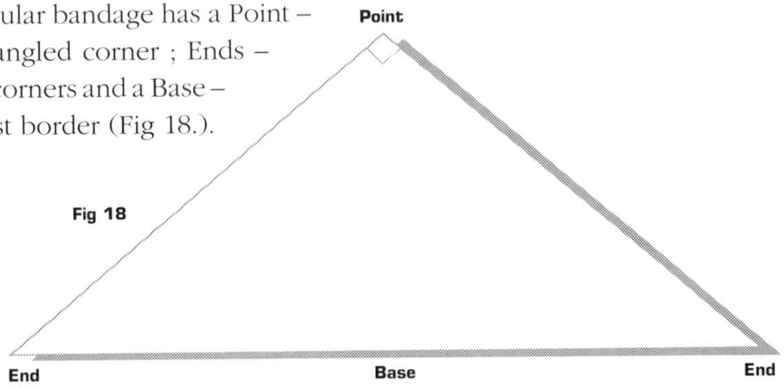

Point

End   Base   End

ARM SLING

This sling is used to support the upper limb with the forearm slightly above horizontal, when the upper limb is injured or in some chest injuries.

Fig 19

● Place an open triangular bandage on the chest with the point beyond the elbow of the injured side and an end over the opposite shoulder. Carry this end round the neck to the front of the shoulder of the injured side. Support the forearm on top of the bandage with the casualty's hand slightly above the level of the elbow (Fig 19.).

● Carry the lower end up over the forearm and hand and tie the ends so that the knot lies in front of the shoulder of the injured side.

● Fold the point forward and pin to the front of the bandage at the elbow (Fig 20.). If no pin is available, twist the fold at the point and tuck it between the bandage and the front of the arm.

Fig 20

● Place an open triangular bandage over the limb with the point beyond the elbow and one end a short distance over the shoulder of the uninjured side (Fig 21.).

Fig 21

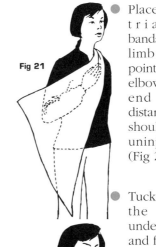

● Tuck the base of the bandage under the hand and forearm.

● Carry the lower end across the back and tie the ends so that the knot lies in front of the shoulder of the uninjured side (Fig 22.).

Fig 22

● Tuck the point between the forearm and the front of the bandage. Pin the fold formed by doing this to the bandage on the lower part of the arm (Fig 23.). If no pin is available tuck the fold over the top of the forearm.

Fig 23

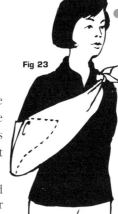

ELEVATION SLING

This sling is used to support the upper limb with the hand at the opposite shoulder, when the hand is injured, or in some shoulder or chest injuries.

● Place the limb of the injured side on the chest with the finger tips at the opposite shoulder.

IMMOBILISATION OF LIMBS

UPPER LIMB

Fractures at the shoulder or in the hand:

- Sit the casualty down.
- If hand injured, protect with soft padding.
- Support limb in Elevation Sling (see p63).
- Place soft padding between limb and chest (Fig 24.).

- Secure limb to chest with broad bandage applied over the sling (Fig 25.).
- Check circulation and sensation in limb at 10 to 15 minute intervals.

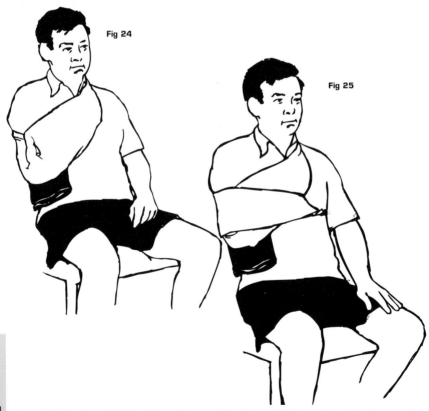

Fig 24

Fig 25

Fractures in arm or forearm:

- Seat the casualty comfortably.
- Support limb in Arm Sling (see p62).
- Place soft padding between arm and chest. If forearm is injured, cradle it in soft padding (Fig 26.).

- Secure limb to chest with broad bandage applied over sling avoiding fracture site (Fig 27.).

Fig 27

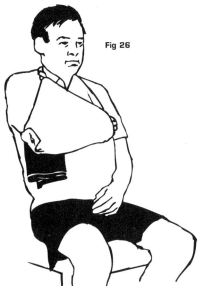

Fig 26

- Check circulation and sensation in limb at 10 to 15 minute intervals.

If elbow cannot be bent without increasing the pain, or the casualty is lying down:

- Make casualty comfortable lying down.
- Support injured limb against trunk (Fig 28.). /continued...

Fig 28

Place broad bandages:

- Under waist and slide upwards so that it will be at the arm above the fracture site.
- Under waist and slide downwards so that it will be round the forearm.
- Under knees and slide upwards so that it will be round the wrist and hand.
- Place sufficient soft padding between limb and trunk so that any space is filled.
- Tie bandage round wrist, hand and body.
- Tie bandage round arm and body.
- Tie bandage round forearm and body (Fig 29.).

- Arrange transport by ambulance to hospital as a stretcher case.
- Check circulation and sensation in limb frequently.

Fig 29

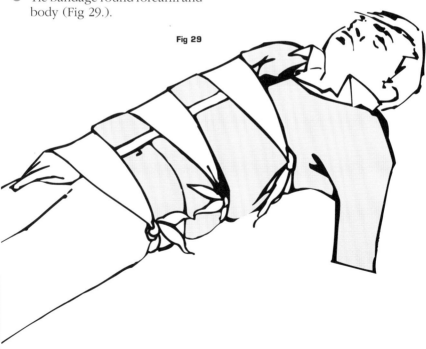

LOWER LIMB

If ambulance is expected quickly:

- Steady and support limb by hand at joints above and below fracture site (Fig 30.) or place cushions or rolled blanket, rug etc at side of limb to steady it.

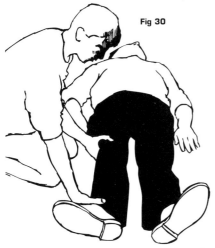

Fig 30

If arrival of ambulance will be delayed:

- Continue support of limb. Use four broad bandages, place them under ankles and knees, above and below site of fracture (Fig 31.).

Fig 31

- Place adequate soft padding between limbs at knees and ankles and fill hollows between legs.

- Bring uninjured limb to side of injured limb.

- If it is necessary to adjust position of injured limb, apply gentle traction at foot before moving it.

- While support is maintained apply bandage at ankles in figure eight round ankles and feet.

- Apply broad bandage round knees, then above and below site of fracture. Tie knots on uninjured side (Fig 32.).

If thigh bone is fractured, bandages are tied as above with the bandages above and below fracture site in thigh.

Check circulation and sensation in limb at 10-15 minute intervals.

Fig 32

CERVICAL COLLAR

- While the casualty's head is being supported, fold newspaper to about ten cms wide.

  Fig 33

- Fold this paper round neck from the front so that it supports the front and sides of the chin (Fig 33.).

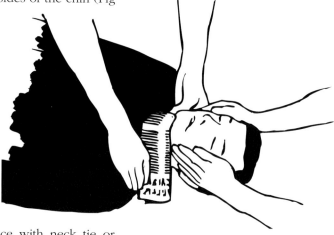

- Tie in place with neck tie or other means available (Fig 34.).

  Fig 34

- The initial manual support of the head should be continued until the ambulance arrives.

ICE
(cooling therapy, cryotherapy)
PURPOSE

Applying ice or other cool materials (eg cold water) is useful in treating acute injuries. It will minimise the bleeding and swelling which occur in such injuries. It will also reduce pain.

METHOD OF APPLICATION

Ice can be obtained from any source, eg from a domestic freezer, and crushed to a convenient size. The skin should be protected by a towel or other material placed over the part. The ice pack should be large enough to cover the affected area and should be applied for only 15 to 20 minutes. Repeat every two hours through the day. Proceed with any further treatment as appropriate.

ADDITIONAL NOTES

The athlete must not  return immediately to the sport as the apparent severity of the injury might be reduced by the pain relieving effect of the ice. To limit the damage:

- Rest - the injured part for 24-72 hours.
- Elevate - whenever possible but especially at night.
- Support - during the day with an elastic bandage.

THE TRAINER'S MAGIC SPONGE

The "magic sponge" and bucket of water must never be used to clean damaged or infected skin. It is therefore easier to use disposable swabs and dressings which can be discarded immediately after use - **use once and discard safely.**

PAIN RELIEVING AEROSOLS

These products have only a brief cooling effect and are expensive for what they achieve.

COMPRESSION BANDAGING

PURPOSE

The use of compression bandaging will inhibit swelling and, in doing so, may reduce the effect of an injury.

METHOD OF APPLICATION

The bandage should be as broad as possible and certainly no less than five cms in width. Place the injured part in a comfortable position. If available, a roll of cotton wool should be wrapped around the part and then the bandage applied over the cotton wool, starting away from the trunk and working towards it. The bandage should be firm enough to prevent movement and maintain even pressure over the part. It should not, however, restrict the circulation nor cause the patient any pain. If available, a crepe bandage should be used.

ADDITIONAL NOTES

The compression bandage should be removed at least every hour for five to ten minutes to allow the circulation to be maintained. It must be removed before sleeping.

ADHESIVE STRAPPING

Strapping should only be applied by those trained in its use.

PURPOSE

Adhesive strapping is used to limit joint movements which cause pain. It should not be used to allow activity which would otherwise be inadvisable and could aggravate an underlying injury.

METHOD OF APPLICATION

IMPORTANT - Enquiry should always be made about possible allergy to adhesive materials and the limb shaved before applying tape. Alternatively, the skin and hair can be protected by a single layer of bandage.

Depending on the area, different widths and materials are used eg in the thigh, 5.0 to 7.5 cms wide elastic strapping should be used, whereas for the ankle 2.5 cms non-elastic strapping is better. As a general rule, strapping should not be wound round the part but longitudinal strands placed on either side of a joint.

HANDLING AND TRANSPORT

In sporting injuries a casualty will often be outdoors in inclement conditions. The casualty must be protected from the weather. After carrying out initial First Aid procedures, in the absence of contra-indications eg spinal injury, the casualty should be moved to shelter, by stretcher if appropriate.

Fig 35

PLACING BLANKET UNDER CASUALTY

- Fold blanket to suitable thickness, bearing in mind that when lying on damp ground more insulation is required below than above.
- Roll folded blanket from side to centre.
- Place rolled edge of blanket close to casualty's side; the injured side if injuries are on one side. Kneel, with assistants if available, at other side of casualty (Fig 35.).

Fig 36

- Gently turn casualty on to his side away from the blanket and support him on his side (Fig 36.).
- Lift blanket to casualty, placing rolled edge close to casualty's back.
- Gently turn casualty on to his back on the blanket. Tilt casualty sufficiently to opposite side to allow the blanket to be unrolled from under him (Fig 37.).
- Settle casualty comfortably on the blanket.

Fig 37

71

72 LOADING STRETCHER USING FOUR PEOPLE

LOADING A STRETCHER USING FOUR PEOPLE

Before using a stretcher it should be tested by lifting an uninjured person of at least the same weight as the casualty.

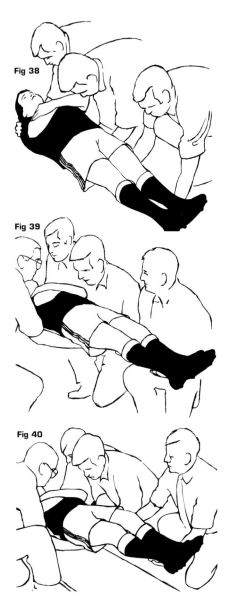

- The opened stretcher should be placed in line with the casualty's head. Three people should kneel on their left knees facing the casualty's left side at shoulders, hips and knees.
- Forearms should be placed under the casualty. The person at the top supporting the head and shoulders, the middle person supporting the small of the back and hips and the third person supporting the thighs and legs (Fig 38.).
- The First Aider in charge should kneel on the casualty's right side facing the chest, and provide additional support to the shoulders and trunk by grasping the wrists of the persons opposite.
- When the First Aider in charge gives the order to "lift", the casualty should be raised slowly and evenly on to the right knees of the three people on the left (Fig 39.). The stretcher is now placed below the casualty by a bystander or the First Aider in charge.
- On the order to "lower", the casualty should be gently and evenly lowered on to the stretcher by all four people (Fig. 40).

Fig 38

Fig 39

Fig 40

LOADING CASUALTY ON 'POLE AND CANVAS' STRETCHER

- Place the open stretcher alongside the casualty (on the injured side if injuries are on one side). Withdraw the pole
- Roll the canvas from side nearest casualty to centre.
- Proceed as for placing blanket under casualty until casualty is lying on the stretcher canvas.
- Gently re-insert pole into sleeve of canvas.

CARRYING A STRETCHER

A stretcher is best carried by four people, except through narrow doorways, with the casualty's feet forward and the person in charge at the front right handle.

- The bearers should stand close to the stretcher, grasping the handles with their inner hands, and keeping their arms straight. The stretcher must be kept level while being lifted, carried and lowered.

- The bearers should move together on command, stepping off with the foot nearest the stretcher and walking with a short flat-footed step to carry the casualty smoothly (Fig 41.).

- In the absence of a stretcher, a conscious casualty with a relatively minor ankle or foot injury can be carried to shelter by a two handed seat (Fig 42. and Fig 43.).

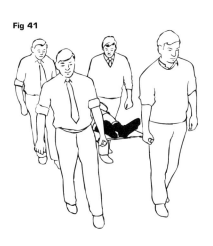

Fig 41

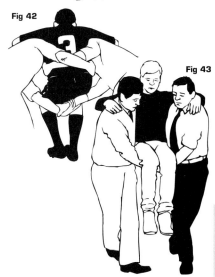

Fig 42

Fig 43

LIFTING OF A CASUALTY FROM WATER

(eg From a Swimming Pool or on to a Boat.)

If the casualty is suspected of having a neck injury, he should ideally be supported horizontally eg on a board, floated to shallow water if possible, with head held in line with the trunk - see spinal injury (p34), then lifted out of the water horizontally with good support. If there is no reason to suspect a spinal injury the casualty should be removed from the water without delay.

FIRST AID EQUIPMENT

All individuals participating in sport, as well as sports coaches, clubs and associations, should have their own First Aid kit. The appropriate equipment will vary with the activity under consideration. An individual spending one hour a week jogging will require a minimum of equipment mainly designed to look after the feet, whereas a rugby or football club will require equipment for muscle, tendon and joint injuries as well as cuts and grazes.

Certain basic facilities should be available for all activities:

- Access to a telephone.
- Dressings for wounds and grazes.
- Disposable gloves.
- Antiseptic solution.
- Bandages.
- An eye pad.
- A supply of clean water.
- A good pair of scissors and safety pins.
- Ice or re-usable ice packs.

In addition, further equipment may be made available but should only be used after individuals have received adequate training:

- Inflatable and rigid splints.
- Neck collar.
- Stretcher.

It is important to repeat at this point that individuals, coaches and clubs have a responsibility to maintain the first aid equipment. There is nothing worse than having an injury to deal with and going to the first aid cupboard and finding that it is bare.

Section 5

RETURNING TO SPORT

Injuries frequently recur - often as a result of incorrect advice or treatment, or because return to full activity was too soon. The period of rehabilitation starts as soon as the injury has occured, and the importance of correct immediate treatment has already been discussed. If medical advice has been sought, the doctor or physiotherapist will normally oversee the initial phase of rehabilitation and should be consulted before full training is resumed.

The first few days after an injury will involve a period of total rest of the injured part, but it is often possible to undertake some activity in order to maintain general fitness. For example, if you have a leg injury, you will normally be able to carry out an upper body exercise programme or non weight-bearing activity such as swimming.

A general fitness programme should be maintained while **gradual** progress is made to restore function in the injured part. For example, after a leg muscle injury, the following steps should be taken:

- Gentle stretching to the point of discomfort (not pain).

- Gentle muscle exercises, slowly increasing the range through which the muscle is used.

- Light weight training.

- Practising technical skills at a slow pace.

- Gradually increasing demands can then be made - such as striding, three quarter pace sprinting, sprinting, changes of direction.

- Participation in full training should precede return to competition.

During the recovery programme it is important not to exercise beyond the point of pain.

RUDLING

It is better to take a little longer to return to full activity than to risk a recurrent or second and more serious injury, because of a lack of patience or trying to overcome a pain barrier. The programme is nearing completion when there is no longer pain, swelling or local heat; when full range of movement and full power of the muscle group has been restored.

The use of strapping is very controversial when an athlete is recovering from an injury. It can be used very successfully to support ligaments after a sprain. It should not be used to enable activities to be carried out which would otherwise cause pain. Generally, strapping should be used for a very limited period to support a joint.

All athletes should be subjected to a fitness test before returning to vigorous or competitive activity. This type of functional test cannot be carried out in the medical room for it must simulate the type of pressures that will be incurred in the competitive/ real situation. To devise such a test requires a comprehensive knowledge of the sport and a ruthless objectivity in assessing the performer's chances of completing the competition/activity without injury.

Athletes often lose confidence when they are injured. This is a particular problem if an athlete should break down a second time because of a poorly supervised treatment and re-training programme.

It is vital that during the rehabilitation phase they continue to be involved with the sport as far as possible. They need plenty of support and encouragement - particularly from the coach - and, in the case of younger participants, from the parents.

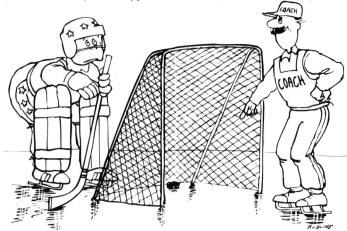

Section 6

WHAT NEXT?

80 AGENCIES AND ORGANISATIONS

WHAT NEXT?

This manual and the accompanying course give a general introduction to the steps which can be taken to avoid sports injuries and, when they arise, on how best to provide immediate safe treatment and care. The purpose of this section is to identify a number of agencies and courses where coaches, parents and others can receive more detailed information on selected elements of this manual. The following are suggestions only and by no means represent an exhaustive list.

AGENCIES AND ORGANISATIONS TO CONTACT

National Sports Councils

The Scottish Sports Council
Caledonia House
South Gyle
Edinburgh
EH12 9DQ

The Sports Council for Northern Ireland
House of Sport
2A Upper Malone Road
Belfast
BT9 5LA

The Sports Council
16 Upper Woburn Place
London
WC1H 0QP

The Sports Council for Wales
National Sports Centre for Wales
Sophia Gardens
Cardiff
CF1 9SW

Coaching

The National Coaching Foundation
4 College Close
Beckett Park
Leeds
LS6 3QH

The British Institute of Sports Coaches
2 College Close
Beckett Park
Leeds
LS6 3QH

VOLUNTARY ORGANISATIONS/OUTDOOR CENTRES 81

Voluntary First Aid Organisations

St Andrew's Ambulance Association
St Andrew's House
Milton Street
Glasgow
G4 0HR

St John Ambulance
1 Grosvenor Crescent
London
SW1X 7EF

The British Red Cross Society
9 Grosvenor Crescent
London
SW1X 7EJ

National Outdoor Training Centres

Glenmore Lodge National Outdoor Training Centre
Aviemore
Inverness-shire
PH22 1QU
(Also contact address for First Aid courses organised by the British Association of Ski Patrollers.)

Plas y Brenin The National Centre for Mountain Activities
Capel Curig
Gwynedd
North Wales

Holme Pierrepont National Water Sports Centre
Adbolton Lane
Holme Pierrepont
Nottingham
NG12 2LY

The Northern Ireland Centre for Outdoor Activity
Tollymore
Bryanford
Newcastle
Co Down
BT33 0PT

Plas Menai The National Watersport Centre
Llanfairissgaer
Caernarfon
Gwynedd
LL55 1UE

Cumbrae National Water Sports Training Centre
Burnside Road
Largs
Ayrshire
KA30 8RW

Accident and Prevention

The Royal Society for the Prevention of Accidents
Cannon House
The Priory
Queensway
Birmingham
B4 6BS

Scottish Accident Prevention Council
Slateford House
53 Lanark Road
Edinburgh
EH14 1TL

Special Needs

British Sports Association for the Disabled
The Mary Glen Haig Suite
34 Osnaburgh Street
London
NW1 3ND

The United Kingdom Sports Association for People with Mental Handicap
30 Phillip Lane
Tottenham
London
N15 4JB

The Scottish Sports Association for the Disabled
Fife Sports Institute
Viewfield Road
Glenrothes
K6 2RA

Federation for Sports Association for the Disabled (Wales)
Sports Council for Wales
Sophia Gardens
Cardiff
CF1 9SN

Health Education

Health Education Authority
Hamilton House
Mabledon Place
London
WC1H 9TX

The Scottish Health Education Board
Woodburn House
Canaan Lane
Edinburgh
EH10 4SG

Water Safety

Royal Life Saving Society UK
Mountbatten House
Studley
Warwickshire
B80 7NN

FURTHER PUBLICATIONS

ST ANDREW'S AMBULANCE ASSOCIATION
ST JOHN AMBULANCE
THE BRITISH RED CROSS SOCIETY

- The First Aid Manual

SCOTTISH SPORTS COUNCIL

- Mountaincraft and Leadership
- Advisory Booklets:
  - Injuries and Sport
  - Drugs, Doping and Sport
  - Infections and Sport
  - Medical Advisory Services and Sport
  - Dangerous Exercises and Sport
- Advisory Posters:
  - Concussion
  - Watch your Mouth
  - Hypothermia
  - Warm-Up
  - Dangerous Exercises
  - Ice and Sport
  - Hygiene and Sport
  - Wounds and Sport

NATIONAL COACHING FOUNDATION

- Introductory Study Packs (book and video):
  - The Body in Action
  - Safety and Injury
- Coaching Handbooks:
  - Physiology and Performance
  - Safety First for Coaches

FURTHER PUBLICATIONS/FURTHER COURSES 85

NATIONAL COACHING FOUNDATION

⬤ **Books:**
- ⬤ Fitness for Sport
- ⬤ Nutrition for Swimming

ROYAL LIFE SAVING SOCIETY (RLSS)

⬤ **Books:**
- ⬤ Lifesaving
- ⬤ Resuscitation and First Aid
- ⬤ Teaching water safety: a project approach
- ⬤ Boat handling

BRITISH ASSOCIATION OF SKI PATROLLERS

⬤ **Manual and Workbook:**
- ⬤ Outdoor First Aid and Safety

FURTHER COURSES

ST ANDREW'S AMBULANCE ASSOCIATION
ST JOHN AMBULANCE

THE BRITISH RED CROSS SOCIETY

⬤ **First Aid Course**

SCOTTISH SPORTS COUNCIL

⬤ **Home Learning Course:**
- ⬤ Safety and Injury

NATIONAL COACHING FOUNDATION

- **Home Learning Courses:**
  - Sports Physiology*
  - Structure of the Body*
  - Sports Mechanics*
  - (* In conjunction with the Scottish Sports Council)
- **Key Courses:**
  - Nutrition and Sports Performance
  - Developing Endurance
  - Developing Strength and Speed
  - Developing Flexibility
- **Advanced Workshop:**
  - Training for Peak Performance

NATIONAL OUTDOOR TRAINING CENTRES

Glenmore Lodge (Scotland)
Plas y Brenin (England)
Tollymore (Northern Ireland)
Plas Menai (Wales)

- **Selected Courses On:**
  - Outdoor Safety and First Aid

ROYAL LIFE SAVING SOCIETY (RLSS)

- **Selected Courses, Including:**
  - Lifesaving
  - Resuscitation
  - Open Water
  - Diploma

ACKNOWLEDGEMENTS

The Scottish Sports Council, National Coaching Foundation and St Andrew's Ambulance Association would like to thank the following individuals for their major contribution toward the writing of the course handbook:

Mr Donald Macleod, Consultant Surgeon, St John's Hospital, Livingston

Mr Jimmy Graham, Consultant Surgeon, Western Infirmary, Glasgow

Dr Ian Pinkerton, Chairman, St Andrew's Ambulance Association

Dr Jim Junor, Chief Medical Officer, St Andrew's Ambulance Association

Their sterling work has ensured that the contents meet the requirements of the three voluntary aid organisations, St John Ambulance, St Andrew's Ambulance Association and The British Red Cross Society, and are therefore applicable throughout the British Isles. The illustrations were drawn by **Archie Shanks** and **William Rudling**.

Index

NOTES